BRROOP

Kris Rhodes

First Printing, 2015

ISBN :9780692542958

Grip and Grin Press
1524 E Ohio St
Indianapolis, IN 46250
gripngrin@outlook.com

Thank you Jessica.

Contents

Weird Fictional Poems

In Reverse, We Do Not Die

In reverse, we do not die.
We coalesce; from dust
to mud to flesh.

A thousand bits of ghost
collapse--to fuel
a sudden breath.

Periphery

the legs
thrice jointed
folded soft
against a white
palpitating body
that hints at future
serration and sheen
on black
I shouldn't do this
but I am reaching out
just almost barely able
to stroke the thing the mouthparts
appear so soft they bury
its head into my thumb
I can feel what it's doing
it's in my knuckle first.

periphery seems
closer now
the world hugs
my face from behind
the details of its arms
apparent
the things in front
too far to touch.

What's Inside

Inside my gut
there's a big bullfrog.
He rumbles a ribbit
he fires his fat tongue
(through my belly button)
to catch and kill
a fly
or a flower
or a dancing squirrel.

Something Useful With Their Time

"I cannot do the same thing twice"
complained the heap, the pile of mice.

"Whenever I try,
a part of me moves,
puts me out of place, creating
something new where
I had wanted it dead
purely formal instead."

(An ample example:
the cruise I refuse.
I try to comply, but
my wiggle-mouse mouth
says "That's last year, dear,"
I smile a while.

        One of me runs up
        her pants. She quakes
        and it dawns; I've wasted
        my only grin.)

    A Denial
    I will not believe her
        gone.

2.
She never was, she never was
  and so she cannot leave.
Her ship will sail, her ship will sail
  but I shall never grieve.

*From the Medical Officer's Report
 .Subject consists of numerous normally
     independent organisms.

.Subject shows apparent coordination
    of intention. Organisms appear
    identical to the common mouse.
.Subject reports inability to repeat self
.Theory: Subject, a communal super-
    organism, moved by evolutionary
    forces not to compete with self.
    Repeated efforts selected against.
    Always something new when old
    was always best.
.Observation: Subject obsesses over an
    incident (fictional?) involving a
    woman, a boat, and inordinate
    bouts of shaking. Subject relives
    incident repeatedly, in contradiction
    of prior claims.
.Note: Communal organism is the
    composer of this report.

We see the seizure
   see the seas
            her fancy knees
        bent to her teeth.
We've been here before, each of us running
              away running like

     gravy, gravy
     on her dress.

       She's going to slap,
           to splash her slip,
               to slip the ship.
We cannot allow her to bow.

After Alice-In-Wonderland

His girlfriend's hair became his country;
her middle ear, his home.
He now begins each day
with supplication, adoration
directed at the eardrum.
The eardrum never moves.

He got the potion
and she the cake.
For months they pretended
but she became too big for the house,
he too small.

For a while he lived perched
on her shoulder while she hunted.
She joined social groupings of giants.
This could only last for so long.

He knows now that all the giants
have little ones like him, scrambling
through hair, finding each other,
wondering at the giants' world
they see hinted on the horizons
of the arms of their hosts.

He should search for such a crowd,
help them build a city
of flakes of skin,
abandon and rebuild
as Wonderland
continues to progress.

The giants will grow too large
for the planet, the atmosphere
sticking to them

while they suffocate.
By then, he calculates,
little ones like him
will be too small to see anything
but quarks,
and you can't see quarks.

Incident During the Slow Trek of the Muon G Minus Two (a Commemoration)[1]

The Muon G Minus Two
done up in lights
for visibility
crawls down main street
on the back of a truck
labeled "wide load,"
for the Muon G Minus Two
is wide, so wide
it threatens the buildings
on either side, but this
is part of the thrill.

It is early,
it is still dark,
everyone took off work
for this. They unfold
lawn chairs, the sidewalk
now a breakfast table
abutting the slowest
smallest parade
in the history of ever.

Garrison Keillor stands up,
"Here's a poem...!" he says,
and reads in *Keillor voce*
a work of Whitmanesque
celebration, on themes
of progress and of work and of
life lived to the full e'en
as it may be a thing passing by.

---

[1] The Muon g-2 is a subatomic particle storage ring which was moved over roads and over the Great Lakes, from New York to Illinois, during the summer of 2013. See: http://muon-g-2.fnal.gov

Cheers and flags
as the Muon G Minus Two
passes, careful not to
bend even a single millimeter,
careful not to crush
the uniformed men
removing rocks
covering potholes
for the sake
of the Muon G Minus Two.

A boy named Cody,
saw how the fight began.

Said one man:
"They're usin' it to
shoot at North Korea
or something ain't they?"

"No no, don't you read?
It's a particle accelerator.
Like, science and stuff."

"The hell do I care about
a particle accelawhatever?"

The other, younger, replied,
"This is history, man, like, we're touching
God here, and you're all 'North Korea!'
That's what they want you to think about!
North Korea is nothing. This is reality
breaking through!"

"Boy," the first voice rises
"I'll break through your face!"

And the younger flipped
the elder off. (Both were drunk.)

As the contretemps began
Cody took cover behind
a lawn chair and the ladies
tried to separate the two.
Then a man in a cape fell
from the sky, cracked
the sidewalk, yelled
at the men to stop.

That is how it happened.

As he was wedging them apart
the Muon G Minus Two
suprised its handlers something fierce
by popping open
like a tank--which it was not--
and it was not supposed to have
a hatch--but anyway
it popped open
and something like a woman
with green skin rose out,
her fingers sliding across
a sheet of glass. Parts
of the Muon G Minus Two
that were not moving parts
began to move.

After a rush of random,
their placement resolved
to clearly point at
the encaped man.
"I have you now!" she screamed.

From behind his lawn chair
Cody was terrified
as everyone ran.
Like Mr. Cape, Cody
was utterly frozen, went
completely white because
this was perfect. This was
exactly how it was
supposed to be.

Merry Christmas!

Merry Christmas, you crazy face of a clown
that laughs at me, that always stares down
at me from the mountain, a face made of stone.
Crazy clown face, I know I am never alone.

Merry Christmas, suit of clothes that walks by itself
following folks in a great show of stealth
coming close to our ears as we go on our way.
Suit of clothes, come and dance! Suit of clothes! Come and play!

Merry Christmas you god-awful sucker-face slime
reposed on the sidewalk in the chillest of climes.
I don't think you see me. I always drive past
with my hands on my face and my feet on the gas.

Merry Christmas, O cosmic and starry machine
who fires a laser that transmits obscene
information to thingybobs placed in my brain.
O Machine! I am able! For today I am sane.

How Things Will Develop

When we toured the house
there was a potted plant
on the mantle. We knew that trick
and the plant had nothing
to do with our decision.
On the day we began

to move our stuff in,
the plant was gone. You
are innocent, but I know the truth.
The plant has not moved.
It continues to find water
and new pockets of soil

in technically adequate amounts,
the sagging unnoticeably slow.
The children will move on,
we will take inventory, and the plant
will be finished with its wilting.
You will say something truly kind to me

as you leave.
We'll handle it
like grandparents.

The Homunculus Talking

"Does our dear auto
glance left or right
when shoving past
his neighbors?
Of course not.
That's for the homunculus
inside," he said.
"So you tell me.
Why take in the skyline
when I march around,
collecting trash?"

I was not sure how this applied.
So he continued:

"Think about the waves.
When they splash. All the
you know, the droplets.
If you knew the shape of the wave..."
(here he made some gestures)
"...perfectly, you'd know each droplet,
each path, each one's shape,
and you'd see."

"See what?"

"The homunculus inside," he said.
"It's the same one every time
thrown in different directions."

"Ahhhh...... but.......
Isn't a homunculus, like,
a man? Or manlike?"

"Yeah yeah, yeah yeah."

16

The way he looked at me
was like I'd stolen his candy
and the candy was poisoned.
He would like to have warned me,
but was too amused to bother.

I said,
"I'm not sure you've got this right."

Then, pointing, you'd think directly at
me, but actually off to the right,
his hand a little floppy:
"That's the homunculus talking!
That's the homunculus talking!"

Your People are so Strange

The shores of worlds
crashing together,
the useless screams--
Minds that span galaxies
flickering, demonstrating
there can be no God--
The taste of dark matter
encoding legends
wrought by ancestors
lying spent, crushed
within my gizzards--

I've known these things
and countless others,
have faithfully delivered
the news unto you.
Yet still you seek--What?

Your people are so strange.
Tell me instead of what you know--
your mud and your tongues
and your crises of identity,
your laughing skeptics
your quantum theory
the squirming of my eyestalks
so deep, deep inside your ear canal--

Head of Steam

I have a head of steam.

You can't touch steam
but only pass through
for a bit of warmth, then things start to feel colder.

My head is gaseous.
Vibrations affect me.
So please be careful what you say and how you say it.

I'd love to finish
anything at all
but the wind blows where it will and I have a head of steam.

Imperative Poems

21

Imperative #1

Continue to be victims
of this harmful native
ritual. Have a cold one
on me. Contain more
carcinogens than normal
cigarettes. Remember.
Remember. Speculate
that the cause of the blast
is unknown. Please remain
standing. Put your right
hand in. Multiply line
three. Store in a cool
dry place. Accept terms
of surrender only if
immunity is granted.
Do not masturbate
until instructed. Move
the first letter to the end
of the word. Replace
the seventh spatula.

Imperative #2

Sometimes show a higher co-
efficient than the lesbian-
hispanic population. Cat-
o'-nine-tails if he is smart-
alec. Plain, mustard only.

Imperative #3

Fruit twenty-one trees.
Spam a ton of folders.
Train the tracks to hope.
Mic the commentator.
Unmic the Slovene.
Mountain these up.
Unhandle a slurp of this
for me. Decide those in.
Sleep a crust, erstwhiley.
Drink his face quick
before he spills again.

Imperative #4

Be the change you wish to see
over there for me while I finish
typing would you be a dear?

Prescription (Imperative #5)

When next you feel
the aforementioned ache
take my advice: concentrate

on the throb, the burn,
notice it still hurts but
you don't mind so much.

Now examine the effect
itself. Apply it once more.
Concentrate, the hurting-

but-not-minding beginning
now to fade. Think about
how you don't mind me

being so right but you
kind of do. Afterwards,
call me up with all your

questions
and comments.

Imperative #6

Think about what it means
for a bathroom to be perfect,
because that's the thing we noticed.

Remember that during our long embrace
the celebration took this form: "The bathrooms,
Honey, the bathrooms are perfect."

Aphoristic Poems

Transient

This stream of piss
as I wiggle my dick.
Such calligraphy!

Papyrus

An empty sheet.
I've waited
long to write
my love upon your skin.

At the Conclusion of a Game of Go

A final stone;
the rain falling outside.
Inside, the thunder.

Inside the Something the Egg

We never have to see
again, just clutch

our heads together.
Whisper--

Eyes closed. We know.

Poetry and Logic

Precise language
which will not be
uttered colloquially.

Keeping Vigil

So carefully
the mountain ignores me.

How can I steal
such a gift?

a paragraph a day a paragraph
a day despair despair hope despair

Other Poems, Almost None of Them Confessional

Morning of

such clarity:
to have not even
eyes, the world
too open, no holes
just insides never
ending. My dearest
children,

> you ran away
> too soon for me
> to fail you, for me
> to take you in,
> to make you mine,
> pale, thin,

unmoving this transparent
morning.

On Internalism, Externalism and the Obtaining of Relations

I quantify over the domain of gazes
and I define a relation over that domain such that
"they meet" is true if and only if they meet.
Let us call the obtaining of this condition "M."

Now,
it is possible (in the epistemic sense)
that M obtained, that day:
you stepped away,
forgot your friends,
looked around at other things.

Shall we say that, at that instant,
my mental state's description
included the notion of M *de re*?
Or was it merely *de dicto*?

I Signed the Papers This Morning. All of Them Will Die.

I made breakfast afterwards, for myself and for
my daughter. (You've met her.) We had a pleasant chat
about her boyfriend. I like him. She is not so sure.
She knows what I've done, I'm certain. And she has her
studies, and her little romances. These things continue.
You are a trusted confidante. We have a long history.
I am glad you are still here with me. In truth
I am surprised.

The Baby and the Milkjug

The baby, the jug,
the kitchen, no clothes.
Let's force it.

Add static, watch
from crooked, flash,
wonder what we saw,
what's
behind
the
frame.

Or go back. Add sound:
family hijinx--Pa sings
the baby prances,
budget's undone,

but we're having fun.
Which shall it be?
Which.
Shall.
It.
Be?

Comments on your Poem

I heard your mother
slept with seven men
before she finally took
responsibility for one
of the results. I wanted
to congratulate you
on that before I begin.
I will be commenting
on style and form, not
on substance, for who
am I to judge, indeed,
to determine whether
there is any substance
here at all? You try too
hard.

How many stanzas
do you need? The tonal
inconsistency is puzzling.
It reads as though each
segment is for a different
audience. Stick with just
a single voice established
in one stanza. Let what
you create with the reader
in that moment stand on
its own. Ha, come to think
of it, this reminds me of
what we were saying about
your mother. Imagine that.

The Last Time You Laughed

I remember, you
grinned, "buttocked?"
You laughed. I remember.

Flesh turns to food. You
and I turned from flesh.
A real transubstantiation

it's been.
The last time you laughed
but we got overbooked

The Best Moments of Our Lives

The wife left me
when our children died.
The house burned down.
They found tumors
in some of my bones.
I peaked in high school.

Cleanliness

1.
I like a messy look.
Ketchup in your hair
and I'm yours.
But do not lay
your shit on me.
These organs are to remain pristine.

2.
Some people have magic fingernails
which develop a layer of dirt underneath
over time no matter which activity
they have been engaged in. Even
sitting there with hands on a table.
The watched nails never become dirty,
but turn your eyes away one time, glance
outside just for a second and brroop.
I am one of these people and it feels
like you're judging me right now.

1.
You take a shower, I'll wash
the sheets. Do not use my toothbrush
until I'm done with it.
No I will not join you
because I don't need to shower
because you,
you beautiful filth,
you touch me in just the right way.

Handprint Seen on Traffic Light

A handprint on the green
light pulls me up short.

My wife's fascination
with hands, also my ex-girlfriend,
this fascination with hands, traced
stamped or otherwise
commemorated.

I do not suggest she left
this handprint, this trace of
"I was here
(and this is what my hand looked like
at the time)."

Was it a man in a hard-hat
aloft on a crane?

Green light goes dark,
the hand disappears,
and now I remember:
a raised hand signals "stop,"
which is what I've done. Another raised hand
adds its half of several claps
to my ear, by my left,
rubs the window, makes sure,
leaves a trace.
Gives up.
I now make a contribution.

Not by hand.
By forehead
I make a mark.
Head in hand.

I do not understand anything.

Rue, Rue, Rue Your Boot

Rue, rue, rue your boot.
Kick the TV screen
Angrily! Angrily! Angrily! Angrily!
Why's the bank so mean?

Show, show, show your boat
To prospective buyers
Cheerfully! Cheerfully! Cheerfully! Cheerfully!
Lawyers are such liars.

Go, go, go for broke.
Nothing left to lose.
Cynically! Cynically! Cynically! Cynically
Fix it all with booze.

Luna

The moth told me this:
For seven days I will be beautiful.
I will fuck and I will die.

During our last argument
the moth told me this
and I answered with my winning grin,

I know what you're really like.

The Eyes Like Tadpoles Swam

The eyes like tadpoles swam
across the face. Or else the face
an ocean swept across the eyes.

But faces and eyes
are fixed, so I conclude
it was me
who swam; he watched.

Letter Received After Twenty-Seven Years of No Contact

Dear Thomas,

I hope this letter finds you well.

Rhoda says to say hello.

NxQ7+.

Best,
-Harold

I See a Disappointment

When I see his ugly whimpering grimace on realizing at the hospital
       that his fun has killed his baby brother
I am reminded of his ugly whimpering grimace two days ago when I
       told him he had lost his favorite watch.
Every happy careless stomp is a happy careless
stomp. Every colliding clump of sand is a colliding
clump of sand. The same face fails the same face
fails.

Compassion Talking

What does it mean--
the sky will fit
inside my eyes
and not my tongue?

What does it mean--
your face will fit
inside my ears
and not my heart?

I shouldn't ask,
but that's compassion
talk. Never again.

Let's see instead--
what tastes the sky?
Let's hear instead--
what hearts your face?

She Escapes with Her Life

Synthetic Version:
trueliesa'slovenlyotardulance
fixhitupbraikmeinafuhryr
smoothruffinitroundacow
needhattherhairymindme

Analytic Version:
Lisa wears a Lyotard, dances, lies and tells the truth in a confusing way, is ambulanced,
   is so lovely, is slovenly, is or has become retarded,
needs fixing, will fix the narrator, has been hit, is upbraiding or being upbraided,
   something is broken, someone needs to be or is being broken in, fury is felt, a furor is occurring, Der Fuhrer has been connoted, there are cows
   around, something is smooth, but also rough, or being roughed up, roughing-it is in, is in it, initiating, there is a finite round, Dachau is
   connoted, need her, hate her, hate her hat, her hat and her hair, there, hey, her hairy mind, reminds me, mind me

The Professor's Perk

I make your grandmother
cry in my office, logic
the topic of her tears.
And she even thanks me
after. You cannot help her.

Christian Rock or Bon Jovi or Something

The radio played
the entire time
perfectly audible.
I hadn't noticed.

You absently turned
into the lot
murmuring

about groceries.
I hate all music.

Poems on More or Less Religious Themes

A River's Supposed to Flow

At the end, mosquitos.
Minnows crowding in,
the algal bloom
a scab.

Trees receive their muddy
bending cracking buggy
life from god knows where.

My Scriptures

The wine--
you rose and did not see the wine.
Thus it toppled.

My book
drank in the living record,
indelible.

Each day
I read anew the jagged splash you left,
foretelling.

The Penitent's Lost Liturgy

The pastor, teacher, prophet or minister shall read the words in **bold**.
The congregation, coven or assembly shall read the words in *italics*.

> **I'm all**
> *for apparent nonsense in general.*
>
> **I do feel**
> *like I get what I get*
>
> **out of this. One from everything.**
> *Possibly*
>
> **the camel/cat adds some.**
> *But it's not clear to me.*
>
> **Still.**
> *If I just delete that part, it does seem.*

The Tongueless Gospel: Selected Pericopes

"A religion to end
all religions" he said.

"So then, the best one of all?"

"Ha ha no, my sillies,
it'd have to be the worst."

They began to take up stones.

....

"You have heard it said,
'Do what I say god damn it,'
but I say to you,
'Every rule is just a tool.'"

"You mean including that one you just made up?"

....

"I'll tell you tomorrow,
I promise. Then you'll know.
You, me, everything I've said,
everything you're doing.
It's a fiction. It never happened,
it never will. The sacred places,
the holy books, sin and salvation:
bullshit. You'll see. Wait for tomorrow.
That's when I'll tell you."

Immediately, they seized him and cut out his tongue.

...

Then he was raised up. They forced him to live,
to live again. And did he laugh? Yes he did.

"You can never make me real!" he cried hilariously,
but the tongueless one could only form the sound
of the secret words, the words spoken from
beginning to end, the words we repeat at every gathering
and in every gesture, the only true words:

"OOO NGA EMVAH MAAECH MUEH WIIIEEEEEAAOW!"

TWELVE BRIEF PASSAGES OF QUESTIONABLE AUTHENTICITY WITH ENIGMATIC COMMENTARY

1.
Purity

Text:
A laborer discovered his fiancé was pregnant even though they had not yet had sexual relations. He was preparing to put her away. But as he walked alone with his dark thoughts, a passing stranger remarked, "This majestic tree holds together the very ground beneath our feet, yet I will never know who planted the seed."

Commentary:
What, do its branches hold up the sky as well?
How many houses could be built from its trunk?
Why is the stranger yammering on about seeds?
Chop it down!

2.
Loyalty

Text:
A child ran away from his parents to take up with the priests of the local temple. The priests were impressed with the young one's knowledge and determination, yet they insisted he must go back to his family. "But my Father is here!" the youth replied. "True enough," they said, "And which of us is your mother?"

Commentary:
I have heard that his family searched desperately for him
and celebrated his return as though he had come back from the dead.
But his elder brother knew better:
no one comes back from the dead.

3.
Striving

Text:
Two men argued over which of them was more enlightened. They agreed to a contest. The one who remained underwater in the nearby river for the longest time must be the most enlightened— for by doing so he will have shown the greatest degree of independence from physical need. A crowd gathered to watch with interest as the two men simultaneously held their breath and submerged themselves into the water. The victor was never seen again.

Commentary:
Nature herself may favor you with a sign--
birds and parting clouds and whispered voices--
yet all this shows is that you have not yet seen victory.
Indeed, victory lies beyond your reach.

4.
Temptation

Text:
A lead disciple took a group of students into the desert, where they fasted for several days. Towards the end of the fast, the lead disciple remarked, "Even the basest stone gives voice to the highest teachings when seen in the right frame of mind." A novice student spoke up, "I am so hungry." The lead disciple replied sternly to the interruption, "You may have your feast when these stones become fish and this desert becomes an ocean." The novice wept at these words, for he did not know how to swim.

Commentary:
Upon their return, the master was amazed.
"How were you all able to walk upon the ocean?
And why did you not bring back fish
for this poor, hungry old man?"

5.
Growth

Text:
The market for mustard was growing, and a farmer decided to begin a test crop. The day after he planted the seeds, he came out to check on them, only to discover in their place a lavish jungle, full of the richest fruits and supporting flocks sufficient to feed his family for generations. The farmer scowled, "This is not right!"

Commentary:
Do you see how bravely I display my cowardice?
If I had even a modicum of sincerity
all mysteries would be revealed.

6.
Obligation

Text:
A man approached a famous teacher, telling him "I fully intend to put all your teachings into practice. But to concentrate on spirit is very difficult for a man like me, with so many debts and no money with which to pay them." The teacher said, "Show me a coin." The man retorted, "I have just told you, I have no money." Then the teacher replied, "Now show me a debt."

Commentary:
That man should pay his obligations in full
before beginning to think of following the teacher's footsteps.
Not until he is an old man, his parents duly buried.
Now show me a spirit.

7.
Love

Text:
Someone asked a great teacher to summarize his teaching. The great teacher, after some thought, replied, "To love oneself should suffice." His hearer was discomfited by this answer, and urged, "Surely some concern for others is important as well." Exasperated, the great teacher clarified: "Simply regard others in the same way and your problem should be solved." Still, his hearer felt the answer was incomplete. "What if someone persists in treating me as an enemy?" The great teacher now shouted, "Why do you insist on harming yourself?"

Commentary:
A man lay sick and dying on the road.
His acquaintances gathered around him and cursed his luck.
His closest friends gathered around him and cursed their own luck.
But his enemy reached out to heal him
so as to torment him the following day.

8.
The End of the World

Text:
A man would preach every day to whoever would listen: "The end of the world is near!" But if anyone began to take him seriously, he would sneer and continue, "How can a thief lament his victims' losses?"

Commentary:
The preacher asks, "How can a thief lament his victims' losses?" What, should the thief steal only from himself?

9.
Resurrection

Text:
A master bid farewell to his students, and died in great agony. Days later his students inquired of him, "What is the body for?" He showed them.

Commentary:
Shall we say this never happened?
Yet see here; you have read it.
Now what is the body for?

10.
Denial

Text:
One of the foremost students of a certain famous master was notorious for insisting he'd never spoken to the man.

Commentary:
We should listen carefully to this insolent student.
He was counted "foremost" for a reason.
His master was out of his mind!

11.
Communion

Text:
A teacher conspired to walk among his students in disguise. Together they all sat to partake of a meal. Not knowing he was there to hear them, his students mocked him mercilessly. He chuckled, for he recognized himself in their caricatures. Then, as the bread came to him, he lunged to a standing position and yanked off his disguise, shouted "Here I am!" with a giant's laugh and tore a great chunk free from the loaf with his teeth. His students were terrified, but he merely passed the bread along.

Commentary:
Only now do the teacher and his students share in fellowship.
Prior to this they must have been great enemies.

12.
Salvation

Text:
A master and grandmaster were conversing. The topic was salvation. The master remarked, "None save themselves. For their every act is self-destruction." The grandmaster replied, "This is true. And also true is this: Self-destruction is self-emptying, and only the empty are filled."

Commentary:
To grasp at salvation is
in itself to fall.
We are already empty.
What more do you need?

Kris Rhodes earned a PhD in Philosophy from the University of California, Irvine in 2011, but has attempted poetry since 1992. Some of his works have been published in *Star*Line,* and some have been featured online at *Songs of Eretz* and at poetrycircle.com.

www.ingramcontent.com/pod-product-compliance
Lightning Source LLC
Chambersburg PA
CBHW070641030426
42337CB00020B/4106